Awareness

Awareness

THE JOURNEY

Donald Fitzgerald

Charleston, SC
www.PalmettoPublishing.com

Character List

Charles

Ashley

Kim

James[YE1] [MF2] [MF3] [MF4]

Occupation; Line cook at fast food restaurant. Come from a single home, being raised by his mom who taught him to be religious. He tries to work hard but always seems to be friends with the wrong people and is always at the wrong place at the wrong time.

Charles

BACKGROUND SHEET

Age: 30
Occupation: Fast food manager
[YE5] [MF6] /modest pay
Lives alone; not many friends

Charles grew up in a foster home with two [YE7] [MF8] siblings. He was adopted as an infant. He was never introduced to the church, Jesus, or his biological family. He was always a troubled kid because he never felt like he fit in anywhere. His trust issues developed when he found out that he was adopted and his brother and sister were not. He has always been a hard worker and has never gotten into any real trouble but has always wondered why his life feels so incomplete. Because of all his trust issues,[YE9] [MF10] he has a hard time connecting with women, so he dates but never has sex with anyone. He never shares these things about himself with anyone, no matter what.

Ashley

Age: 27
Occupation: Hairstylist/modest pay
Lives alone; very popular because
of her occupation

Ashley is an only child who grew up with both of her biological parents who were married to each other. She was introduced to church and Jesus as a child. She has even found a best friend and churchmate in her neighbor Kim. Ashley made the choice to be baptized when she was 12 years old. She has always been a hard worker and a well-adjusted person who can get along with anyone.

She tries to live her life as openly and honestly as possible. She would constantly pray for a happy life when she grew up. To her, this means having a good job that allows her to support herself and have a car to get around, a place of her own, and a loving man to share it all with. Because of her church background, she wants to wait until she's married before having sex. She dates but can't keep a man because of this, and she prays to Jesus, urging him to solve this problem.

Kim

Age: 28
Occupation: Motivational speaker/
life coach/Ashley's prayer partner
Lives alone/stress free and blessed

Kim and Ashley grew up together. They went to the same schools and the same church, and they even got baptized together. Because Ashley did not have any siblings, she and Kim became more like sisters than just best friends.

Kim is a people person, and she always works hard at anything that she does. She always makes sure to put GOD first in everything. She runs the free food center for the church, she's a motivational speaker in the local prisons,[YE11] [MF12] and she tries to spread the good news about the Lord [YE13] [MF14] wherever and however she can. Hallelujah, amen!

Scene One

(At the bus stop, Charles meets Ashley.)
[YE15] [MF16]

Charles: Hi, how are you doing on this fine day?

Ashley: I'm good. How about you?

Charles: I'm okay, [YE17] [MF18] I guess. You look nice today. Ashley: Thanks. You don't look so bad yourself.

Charles: By the way, my name is Charles and your name is?

Ashley: Ashley.

Charles: That's a nice name. It fits you. *(Charles chuckles.)*

Ashley: What's so funny?

Charles: Oh, it's nothing. I'm just laughing at my-self because I can't believe that I'm really having a conversation with such a beautiful woman at a bus stop, that's all. I usually don't approach women this way. There's just something about you that made me want to speak to you.

Ashley: Ooooh. That must mean I'm special.

Charles: Maybe[YE19] [MF20] . So,[YE21] [MF22] can I get your number so that I can call you sometime?

Ashley: Sure, why not, but only if I can get your number too.

(Narrator: Charles and Ashley exchange phone numbers. Ashley wonders where this could lead and if this is God finally answering her prayers for love.)

Ashley: I wonder where this bus is?

(Narrator: As time progresses, Ashley and Charles decide to go on some dates. Eventually, Charles and Ashley become inseparable. They get engaged, and Charles moves into Ashley's apartment. They're in a committed relationship, and Charles and Ashley are completely happy together. Because Ashley has been praying

to God to give her a man who will love her unconditionally, she is overjoyed and thankful to God for everything. Ashley feels that her prayers have been answered, and she has to share her good news with someone, so she calls her best friend and sister in Christ, Kim.)

Scene Two

(Ashley is on the phone with Kim.)

Ashley: Hey, [YE23] [MF24] girl.

Kim: What's going on with you? I haven't heard from you in a while.

Ashley: Nothing much. You got time to talk? I know you be busy [YE25] [MF26] being a life coach and everything. *(Ashley chuckles.)*

Kim: Yeah, girl. I do be running around like a chicken with my head cut off, but I got a few minutes to talk. So, what's on your mind today?

Ashley: I just wanted to touch base with you and let you know that life on this side is going well—from the food that I eat to the clothes on my back—and it's all because of Jesus. He has been soooooo good to me.

Kim: Oh yeah. You sound unusually happy. What's really going on with you?

Ashley: Well, you know I've been praying for God to let me meet the love of my life, right?

Kim: Okay and?

Ashley: Well, I met this guy, and he makes me happy. And I owe it all to Jesus.

*(**Narrator:** Charles walks in and overhears Ashley on the phone. He just stands off in the background, not letting Ashley know that he's listening. As he listens, it sounds like she's talking about some guy or something. So he gets a little closer so that he can hear what she's saying.)*

Kim: I know that's right, girl. In the name of Jesus, God is good all the time.

Ashley: I know. Jesus is my main man, and I love him soooooo much.

Kim: I'm glad you're doing well, girl. I hate to cut this conversation short, but I have to go. You know I have to do God's work. Keep in touch.

Ashley: I will.

(Narrator: *The conversation ends, and Charles can't believe what he just heard. His lady was seriously talking about another guy. He acts as if nothing is wrong and walks in and hugs Ashley, not saying anything about this guy named Jesus who he just heard her talking about.)*

Scene Three

Charles: Hey, babe, were you just on the phone or something? I thought I heard you talking to someone.

Ashley: Yeah, I was on the phone, talking to Kim.

Charles: Oh, okay. What were you two talking about?

Ashley: Nothing much. Just how good life is and how we need to make an effort to keep in contact with each other. That's about it.

Charles: Oh, okay. Well, I'm hungry. What are we having for dinner tonight?

Ashley: I don't know. I really don't feel much like cooking today. How about we order Chinese food or go out to eat or something?

Charles: That sounds good to me. I could eat almost anything right now. We should go to a buffet; that way we can eat whatever we want, and I can eat a lot because I'm starving.

Ashley: That's fine, and that way we'll only have to pay for you to eat one meal. *(Ashley chuckles.)*

Charles: Cool. Let's go eat.

*(**Narrator:** Charles never mentions hearing her talking about this dude named Jesus, but it stays in the back of his mind.)*

Scene Four

(Kim is on the phone with Ashley.)

Kim: Hey, girl.

Ashley: Hey, what's going on with you? You don't sound like your regular self. Is everything okay?

Kim: I just really need someone to talk to right now. You're not busy right now, are you? I just had a bad day today. Other than that, I guess I'm doing okay.

Ashley: What's going on? Do you want to talk about what happened?

Kim: Yeah. That's why I called you because I know that you're not going to be judgmental about my situation.

Ashley: Well, you know I'm always here to listen whenever you want to talk. So, what happened? It can't be that bad.

Kim: Well, you know that I'm a life coach and I travel all over to spread the good word about Jesus and inspire people to do better in their lives, right?

Ashley: Okay. So, what happened?

Kim: Well, I was speaking to a group of middle school kids earlier this morning.

Ashley: Okay. So, what's wrong with that?

Kim: Usually nothing, but this time there were soooo many kids who had such a negative attitude about everything.

Ashley: Really? What was your speech about?

Kim: It was about success and how God will make a way for those who believe in him and in the name of Jesus and work hard all the time and pray for what they need to make it through whatever they're [YE27] [MF28] dealing with.

Ashley: That sounds like a great speech. I wish I was there to hear it. I would have been in the audience like I was in church, shouting "hallelu-jah" and "amen" the whole time. So, what was the problem?

Kim: I didn't feel like there was a problem with my speech until the kids started to boo me because I was talking about Jesus.

Ashley: I can't believe that really happened. I would have panicked and run out. What did you do?

Kim: I just had to call on Jesus and prayed that he would deliver me from this situation. I felt sooooo embarrassed, but I was mostly confused because I couldn't believe that anyone would react like that just from hearing the name Jesus. It was so unbe-lievable to me.

(Charles is in the background, listening to Ashley on the phone.)

Ashley: Well, I'm sorry to hear that you didn't have a good day today. I'm just glad that Jesus was able to help you with your situation. You know that Jesus can do anything. That's why I love him so much. He always seems to be at the right place, at the right time all the time. OMG. I love me some Jesus.

Kim: I know; that's right. That's why I called you—because I knew that you would just listen.

Ashley: That's what friends are for. Call me whenever you need to talk.

Kim: I will. Thanks for listening. Ashley: Anytime!

(Narrator: Ashley hangs up the phone, and Charles walks in. She offers him a hug, but he shrugs her off and walks right past her. Ashley feels like he's acting weird, but she doesn't say anything about it. She figures that maybe he is having a bad day like Kim, and she doesn't want to press the issue with him. After all, she just got off the phone with Kim, and she feels that being helpful to one person a day is enough for her to deal with. So she figures that he would like to be left alone to deal with his own issues. Charles never mentions hearing her talking about this guy named Jesus again.)[YE29] [MF30]

(Narrator: As time goes on, Ashley feels like there is something serious going on with Charles, but she never asks him about it. She just waits for him to volunteer the information and continues to let it go. She goes about her daily routine as if everything is okay.)

*(**Narrator:** While Ashley is walking around acting as if everything is fine, Charles starts to do things such as looking through her purse, phone contacts, drawers, and closet in search of anything that could show him if Ashley is really involved with this guy named Jesus. He is sooooooo irritated that his lady is always talking about this dude.*

Charles gets angrier and angrier as he can't find anything about this dude. So he starts to follow Ashley everywhere she goes. He even starts doing pop-up visits at her job. He begins lurking around and offering to go with her everywhere. Ashley feels like this is weird but starts to like that her man wants to start paying her more attention. He even starts cooking her dinner and surprising her with gifts. Charles' actions please Ashley so much that she becomes overjoyed with the way her life is going. Ashley continues to be thankful to God and Jesus for giving her this great life. Little does she know that Charles is doing these overly nice things [YE31] [MF32] for her only to keep her from feeling like she needs to replace him with this guy named Jesus. Charles feels that he has to do everything in his power to hold on to Ashley because she's the first woman he's ever truly loved and the only person he can trust. Something has to be done to put her relationship with Jesus to an end.)

(Narrator: Charles gets off work early today. He's happy that Ashley isn't there so that he can have time to go through her things before she gets home. He feels that he must have overlooked something about this Jesus dude.)

(Narrator: Ashley gets home and finds Charles going through her stuff and asks him what he's doing and why he is going through her things.)

Scene Five

Ashley: What are you doing, Charles?

Charles: What does it look like I'm doing, Ashley?
Ashley: Why are you going through my things?

Charles: Because I feel like you're [YE33] [MF34] hiding something from me.

(Narrator: Charles is angry with Ashley because she keeps talking about this Jesus dude, but he never mentions this to Ashley. Instead, he just tells her that he feels that he can't trust her.)

Charles: Are you cheating on me, Ashley?

Ashley: NO. Where is this coming from? I thought that everything was fine between us, Charles. What's going on?

(Narrator: Charles ignores Ashley. He calls her a liar and continues to search through her things. Ashley storms out of the room. As she leaves the room, Ashley mumbles something under her breath.)

Ashley: I need to talk to Jesus about this.

> *(Narrator: Charles hears Ashley and follows her out of the room.)*

Charles: You're not going to keep disrespecting me like this, Ashley.

Ashley: What are you talking about, Charles? I can't believe this. Why are you doing this? I haven't done anything wrong. Jesus, help me.

> *(Narrator: Charles runs up behind Ashley and strikes her. Ashley runs for the door. A neighbor hears them tussling and calls the cops. Eventually, Charles is carted off to jail. Ashley is left alone, feeling hurt, abused, and deserted [YE35] [MF36] by Jesus. What a mess.)*

(Narrator: Soon after Charles is carted off to jail, Ashley receives news that her parents were in a horrible car accident, and they didn't survive. She feels that God and Jesus have left her completely alone. There was that confrontation with Charles, and now, her parents are gone. Ashley falls

into a deep depression, so to comfort herself, she turns to drugs and alcohol. She's avoiding Kim's phone calls. She stops going to work. She stops reading her Bible[YE37] [MF38] . She stops going to church. She stops praising and praying altogether. She loses her job, having lost her parents, her friends, and her man. [YE39] [MF40] She has given up on everything.)

(Narrator: *Meanwhile, Charles is in jail awaiting his day in court. While there, he meets an inmate named James who takes an interest in him.)*

Scene Six

<u>[YE41]</u> <u>[MF42]</u>

James: What are you in for, man?

Charles: Dude, why don't you mind your business? James: Look, dude, I'm just trying to be friendly here. If you don't want to talk, that's fine, but you don't have to be rude.

*(**Narrator:** Charles tells James what happened. James listens, speechless. He really can't believe what he's hearing.)*

Charles: You know what? It's not even my fault that I'm here. This is all that dude Jesus's<u>[YE43]</u> <u>[MF44]</u> fault.

James: Hold on. What did you just say?

Charles: You heard me. If Ashley hadn't been so interested in this Jesus dude, then we wouldn't have gotten into it. She was always on the phone talking to her friend about how much she loves that dude and what he does for her—like I'm noth-ing. I couldn't take it anymore. So when I heard her say that she was going to talk to him to my face, I just lost it. I refuse to be disrespected like that, especially when I love her more than life. I can't wait to get out of here so that I can deal with this dude. He ruined my relationship with my lady, and he's not going to get away with this.

*(**Narrator:** James starts laughing. He really can't believe what he's hearing. He has never met anyone so clueless about God. He has just got to be joking or out of his mind, so James decides to offer Charles a Bible.)*

James: Look, man. I understand your situation, and I got this book that might be able to help.

Charles: Look, dude. I don't need no book to help me. The only thing that's going to help me is to apologize to Ashley and let her know how much I really do love her. I also have to deal with this Jesus dude face to face. I have to confront him and let him know that he can't have my lady. This is all his fault.

James: Look, Charles. I really think you might want to check out this book. It really [YE45] [MF46] might shine some light on your situation.

Charles: Look, dude. I know you mean well, but I'm telling you no book will help. I just got to find this Jesus dude and let him know that his relationship with my lady is over.

(Narrator: James is completely shocked by Charles's attitude toward Jesus. He begins to think that, maybe, Charles really has never been introduced to Jesus or the Bible. He has to help this man understand what's going on, so he continues to talk to Charles with the hope that he can get through to him. In the name of Jesus, hallelujah. Amen.)

James: Not to judge your situation, but how do you know your girl will take you back after all of this anyway?

Charles: Because deep in my heart, I know she still loves me, and I'm telling you I'm going to get rid of that Jesus dude. Once I do that, everything will be okay.

James: Not to discourage you, but I doubt that you are going to get rid of Jesus. Trust me. If you would just take some time and read this book, you'll see exactly what I'm talking about.

Charles: What do you mean "I won't be able to get rid of Jesus"? You are acting like you know him or something. And you can stop offering me that book because I'm telling you that no book will help me. We should talk about something else.

James: Only if you promise that you will come somewhere with me tomorrow.

Charles: What are you talking about? We're in jail. Where can we go?

James: There are plenty of things we can do here.

Charles: Like what? Look at these dingy walls?

James: *(James chuckles)*: NO. We can go to the gym. They have a library here. They even have a chapel here. Just because we are here, it doesn't mean that we can't be productive.

Charles: Oh, okay. That does sound interesting, but I got a question.

James: Okay, shoot.

Charles: What is a chapel? Isn't that where folks go to get married? If so, I'm not interested, dude. I'm getting back with my lady after I get rid of this Jesus dude and have this mess cleared up.

(James starts laughing again.)

James: Man, it's not like that. It's hard to explain. How about I show you tomorrow? It starts at about 9a.m[YE47] [MF48] . We can meet up after breakfast and go.

Charles: Cool.

Scene Seven

*(**Narrator:** The following morning, James and Charles meet at breakfast.)*

Charles: You know, James, I talked so much about myself yesterday that I forgot to ask you what you are in for.

James: That's all right. You had a lot on your mind, and my friends tell me that I'm a good listener.

Charles: Well, I want to thank you for that, but it's time for you to tell your story.

James: Well, one night, I was invited to a party, and against my better judgment, I decided to go. Long story short, right after my friend and I arrived at the party, it got raided for drugs. Everyone but me was high, and the cops assumed that it was because I was a drug dealer. I looked around for my friend so that we could explain why we were there at this party, but he was gone.

Charles: Man, that really sounds like a setup.
James: I didn't think of it like that.

Charles: That is messed up. I hope that everything works out so that we both can get out of here quickly because you know that I got to deal with that Jesus dude for real.

James: I can't believe that you're really still talking about doing something to Jesus. You don't even know what you're talking about.

Charles: Look, I'm tired of you defending this Jesus dude. I know you mean well, but I still can't wait to get out of here. I'll have to deal with Jesus my way.

James: You know, Charles, you're right. You are going to have to deal with Jesus on your own.

Charles: I know I'm right. Now ain't it about time for you to take me to check that chapel thing?

James: Man, yeah, let's go. But I have to get my book first.

Charles: Man, oh, man. You just can't stop thinking about that book, can you?

(Charles and James set off for the chapel.)

(Meanwhile, Kim has arrived at the chapel, and she is waiting for the inmates to come down for service. She is feeling nervous because of her last incident at the middle school. Well, here goes nothing.)

Kim: How is everyone doing today? *(No one answers, so she continues.)* I see we have some new faces in the place today. *(No one responds.)* Anyone want to introduce themselves? *(Still, no one responds, so she continues.)*

Kim: Well, I guess I'll go first. Hello, everyone, my name is Kim, and I am a motivational speaker. Does anyone know what that means?

(Okay, Charles is about to snap because he feels like he's being set up. He decides to stand up and say something.)

Charles: First of all, my name is Charles, and I would like to say that although I do understand what a motivational speaker is, I don't feel that I have a need for one. And furthermore, I wouldn't even be here if that Jesus dude hadn't been in a re-lationship with my lady in the first. Tell them what I told you about my situation, James. Go ahead.

Tell them! *(He is screaming and hollering at James to tell everyone his story.)*

(James begins to chuckle. He can't believe that he is being put on the spot like this. So he tells the group what Charles told him the day before about the situation between Ashley and him. He makes sure to explain that Charles believes that Jesus is responsible for the whole problem.)

James: I can't believe you think that Jesus is really a problem and not a problem-solver.

(James starts to shake his head. Kim starts to sense that something is wrong, so she decides to say something.)

Kim: Wait a minute. Did I hear you guys correctly? Are you, Charles, saying that you believe that Jesus would get involved in a physical relationship with your lady to the point that it would cause you and her to have a domestic violence situation that would land you here?

Charles: Yes. That's what I've been saying all along. That dude doesn't know what I'm going to do to him when I get out of here.

James: Charles, I don't know what to say about you, dude. I've tried to tell you that Jesus isn't like that. Did you even read the book that I gave you?

Charles: I told you that book wouldn't help me, so why would I want to read it? And why are you sitting up here taking Jesus's side anyway? You're acting like you know this dude. Do you, and are you not telling me? What's going on here, James?

James: Look, dude, I don't want no problems, but I want you to listen for a minute.

Charles: Okay, shoot.

James: I do know Jesus.

Charles: What!

(Charles snaps and gets extremely violent with James.)

Charles: I knew it. I knew it. I knew it. Is that why you wanted to be cool with me because you know that dude Jesus? Is he in here? Y'all trying to set me up or something? Naw, that ain't going to work, because I'm too smart for all that. I got a plan for that.

(James[YE49] [MF50] tries to explain to Charles about Jesus again. How Jesus died on the

cross for all of our sins. How Jesus loves us no matter what our situation may be. How he would never come between the union of a man and a woman physically. Charles just refuses to listen. He feels that James is defending Jesus and starts hitting him. Guards have to break the two apart and they both end up in the hole.)

(Narrator: Kim is in total shock. She's experiencing déjà vu[YE51] [MF52] . She can't believe what she is seeing. At first, she thought that it was just kids, but now she is seeing that adults don't believe in Jesus either. She's having a hard time believing that there are really people in the world that think that Jesus is the Lord of confusion and destruction. How could this be? What a mess. She is quickly escorted out of the jail. As soon as she is safe, she tries to contact Ashley. She finds it odd that she hasn't heard from her in weeks, so she decides to go to her house to check on her. And besides, after the day she just had, she could definitely use someone to talk to, and who better to listen than Ashley? So she decides to drive straight to Ashley's house. Once Kim gets there, she finds Ashley and her house in a total mess. Liquor bottles, dirty clothes, old food—you name it, you found it. This is out of character for Ashley. Kim approaches her and asks if she's okay and what is going on. She has forgotten all about the day she had at the jail.)

Scene Eight

*Narrator: [YE53] [MF54] Ashley responds,
"Why are you here, Kim? Wasn't it obvious that I
didn't want to be bothered when I didn't answer
the phone when you called?"*

*Kim is thrown off by the attitude that Ashley
is giving her, and she doesn't know quite
how to respond to her. She has never
seen her friend like this. Kim says a short
prayer and proceeds with caution.*

Kim: I just came by to check on you because
I haven't heard from you in a while, and I don't
want us to lose touch again. And from the look
of things around here, I'm glad I did. Look at this
place. What's been going on, Ashley? It looks
like you been going through something serious
over here, girl? Why have you been avoiding me?
Maybe I could've helped you with whatever you've
got going on?

For a moment, Ashley stays silent. Then out of nowhere, she begins to cry hysterically.

Kim approaches Ashley to give her friend a loving hug.

Kim: No need for all of those tears, Ashley girl. Whatever is going on, sister, you know that the Lord will always be there to see you through. In the mighty name of Jesus, amen.

Ashley then becomes angry with Kim and starts yelling at her: You're always going on and on about Jesus and how you think he is going to always be there for somebody. You think you and Jesus got everything figured out, don't you? If only you knew half of it.

Kim: What has changed? You never used to feel this way about the Lord. You used to believe that everything is possible through Jesus and with the love of God.

Ashley: Just stop. If Jesus really cared about me, I really wouldn't be sitting here in the mess that I'm in right now. My life is falling apart.

Kim: What are you talking about, Ashley?

Ashley: Everyone has abandoned me. My man, my parents, and your Lord and Savior, Jesus Christ.

Kim: Now you can stop right there, Ashley. I don't know what has gotten into you, but it is clear that you need some help right now. And the only way that I can think to help is to pray. Let us pray about your situation, Ashley, because prayer always works.

Ashley: No, you need to stop, Kim. It's my life that has fallen apart, and I don't feel like listening to you preach about the goodness of Jesus today. If Jesus was supposed to be so good, why did he let the love of my life hit me and get locked up over a misunderstanding? If Jesus was so good, why did my parents die so suddenly in that brutal car crash a few days later, leaving me alone? Jesus is so sweet and so good that my best friend...

(Narrator: Ashley is crying hysterically and has fallen into a heaping mess on the floor.)

Kim: Your best friend is what? Look, Ashley. I've been trying to contact you for weeks and now what? Your best friend is right here. Wow, sis. You have been dealing with some serious stuff over here, girl. And you really think Jesus wasn't there to help you through any of it? It had to be the

Lord that had me just come over here because you weren't answering, Ashley. If Jesus hadn't sent me to you today, I wouldn't have known what was going on with you, sister. Look, Ashley, you know that no matter what your struggles in life are, Jesus will always make a way for you to get through them. All you have to do is stand firm in your faith and keep pushing forward. You should come back to church.

Ashley: There you go preaching again.

Kim: What do you mean I'm "preaching again," Ashley? There used to be a time when I couldn't drag you out of the church. I know you haven't forgotten how good it feels to be in God's house, just listening to the Word, Ashley.

I'm not preaching to you, sister. I'm just offering a suggestion.

Ashley: I know you're not preaching, Kim. It's just that I've been away for so long that I don't know if the Lord will accept me back after the things that I've done. Look around. You can pretty much see that I've given up and don't deserve forgiveness from Jesus, and you know how judgmental church people can be.

Kim: Ashley, that's pure nonsense. Who cares if church people judge you? You're supposed to go to church for the Lord, not the people. And besides, everyone deserves forgiveness, but we must forgive ourselves first. But may I ask, what do you really think you did wrong? Because all I really heard is what happened to you, and it sounds like most of it was out of your control. If you're blaming yourself for a man hitting you, then I must tell you [YE55] [MF56] that was all on him. That car accident was just that, an accident. What it sounds like is you have been put in some serious situations, and you could have handled things differently. With the help of the Lord, plenty of prayer, and maybe coming back to church, I believe that everything will be okay. Have faith, Ashley. Don't stop praying, and you know the Lord will be there for you. In the Name of Jesus. You'll know when you want to return to church. And remember, it's just a suggestion, and I'm always here for you too.

Ashley: I know. I'm going to think about everything you said, and I'm glad you came by. I really needed you, and I didn't realize it. I know you're not preaching. I have just been having a hard time with everything that's been going on, and I really didn't know where to turn. I've always had a hard time forgiving myself and dealing with loss. I just threw in the towel. But now no more, thanks to you, Kim. You reminded me [YE57] [MF58] that I can turn to the good Lord and Savior Jesus for help getting through anything.

With tears in their eyes, Ashley and Kim hugged.

Ashley: I need some serious help right now.

Kim: You want my help cleaning your house.

Ashley: You know me so well.

Kim: That's what friends are for.

Scene Nine

A month later, after staying in touch with Kim, praying, reading her Bible, and talking to the Lord about forgiving herself and others, Ashley decided to return to church. Amen and amen again.

CHARLES

During his time in the hole, Charles continued to blame Jesus for everything.

I can't [YE59] [MF60] believe that Jesus took the love of my life away from me and made me hit her. I can't believe that Jesus got me locked up in this jail because of that. Me hitting Ashley has to be some kind of misunderstanding that Ashley and I can work out. And now I'm in this hole all because James tricked me. I thought he was my friend but turns out he knows this Jesus dude too. I feel like Jesus is just setting me up. Everybody around me seems to know Jesus but me. What can I do?

He starts to feel like he's in a hopeless situation, so he gets angry and starts throwing everything around the room.

That's when he notices writing on the wall, which says, "DO YOU BELIEVE IN JESUS?" At this point, he really just starts to wonder what is going on here: "Have I completely lost my mind? Now I'm seeing things in writing." This sets him off to the point where he begins hitting the walls. After a few minutes, he stops to calm himself down, enough to see a hole in the wall where he finds a small book titled The New Testament. He picks it up and begins to see that it isn't a normal book and panics. Then he gets curious and begins to feel like maybe, just maybe, he should read this book. The first thing he notices is that it is broken down into chapters named after men, such as Matthew, Mark, and Luke. He finds that to be interesting. So he goes to the beginning of the book and begins to read it.

"And she shall bring forth a son, and thou shalt call his name JESUS: for he shall save his people from their sins.[YE61] [MF62] "

Matt 3:16-17 As soon as Jesus was baptized, he went up out of the water. At that moment heaven was opened, and he saw the Spirit of God descending like a dove and lighting on him. And a voice from heaven

*said, "This is my Son, whom I love; with him
I am well pleased.*

*"John 3:17-21 For God did not send his Son
into the world to condemn the world, but
to save the world through him. Whoever
believes in him is not condemned, but whoever does not believe stands condemned
already because he has not believed in the
name of God's one and only Son. This is the
verdict: Light has come into the world, but
men loved darkness instead of light because
their deeds were evil. Everyone who does
evil hates the light and will not come into the
light for fear that his deeds will be exposed.
But whoever lives by the truth comes into
the light, so that it may be seen plainly that
what he has done has been done through
God. James*

While James is in the hole, he is worried about
Charles. Wondering why Charles hadn't under-
stood what was going on. That Jesus was not some
random dude that would come between him and
his lady. But worse than that, it seems like Charles
really has no clue what Jesus is all about. Are there
really people in the world who don't know God or
Jesus? Is the world really this messed up?

I don't know why I'm so shocked, though. Look
at the situation I'm in. I know better. I even grew

up hearing about the goodness of the Lord, yet I keep finding myself in trouble for no reason. How can I feel like I can help someone else when my life is such a mess? I feel like my relationship with the Lord is on shaky ground all the time because I stay in and out of trouble. Maybe I should just try one more time to give him this book and pray about the situation. If I do that, then maybe the Lord will listen to my prayers and do what is best.

After this manner, therefore pray ye:

Our Father which art in heaven, Hallowed be thy name.[YE63]

"Thy kingdom come. Thy will be done in earth, as it is in heaven." (Matt. 6:10)

"Give us this day our daily bread." (Matt. 6:11)

"And forgive us our debts, as we forgive our debtors." (Matt. 6:12)

"And lead us not into temptation, but deliver us from evil: For thine is the kingdom, and the power, and the glory, for ever. Amen." (Matt. 6:13)

"For if ye forgive men their trespasses, your heavenly Father will also forgive you:" (<u>Matt. 6:14</u>)

"But if ye forgive not men their trespasses, neither will your Father forgive your trespasses." (<u>Matt. 6:15</u>)

Please forgive me, Father, for I know that I am nothing more than an imperfect person. All I want to do is get closer to you, Lord, and follow the right path in life. I know that you are a gracious God, and you answer prayers, and you forgive even people who seem to take your kindness for granted, so I'm praying on bended knees that I'm on the list of people who are among the forgiven. I'd like to pray for a clear mind, a healthy body, wisdom, and the opportunity to do better, Lord. I pray for these things in the name of Jesus. Oh, and God, I want to pray for Charles. I pray that he can finally see that there is nothing but unconditional love where Jesus is concerned, Lord. I sincerely pray all these things in the name of Jesus.

Amen.

I wish I could talk to Charles because I just have to give him this book.[YE64] [MF65]

30 DAYS LATER

After being released from the hole, James and Charles run into each other at breakfast.

Charles: James, I want to apologize to you for my actions because I didn't mean to become so hostile that day. I just felt like I was being set up. The situation with Ashley, then you coming out saying that you know Jesus too. It was a bit much for me at the time. And I had never been to a chapel before.

James: I understand. You were going through some things. And learning about Jesus can be hard, especially when you think everybody around you is against you. So let me give you this book. I promise that it will help you.

Charles: But wait, James, you can keep your book because I found this one when they put me in the hole. I've been reading this the entire time I was there.

James: This is unbelievable. Look at God's work.

They shake hands and give each other a brotherly hug.
    They return to the chapel.

Kim returns to the jail and is escorted back to the chapel. There she is greeted by some of the same faces and a few new ones, so she begins to feel nervous again. So, as usual, she starts with a speech to try to break the ice.

Kim: The last time I was here, there was a lot of miscommunication that led to some violence.

That's when Charles and James walk in unexpectedly. She starts to get really nervous because she sees the two guys that had fought walk into the room. She says a silent prayer but starts to calm down because there's extra security in the room. Charles and James take a seat.

Kim decides to open with a prayer. Maybe this will keep the mood in the room calm.

Kim: Can everyone please stand so that we can open with prayer, please? Charles looks at James and asks, "What is prayer?"

James: It's cool; we'll talk about it later. Trust me, my friend, you have a lot to learn, but first, you have to take baby steps. And the first step is reading the book and coming back to the chapel. So don't flip out. It's not going to be easy, but I'm going to help you.

Charles: You're right. I'll get my head in the game.

(Narrator: And then they stood up
to join everyone in prayer.)

Kim: I'll be reading the daily prayer from Matthew Chapter 6 You:9. If you have a Bible, feel free to read along.

e: This then is how you should pray:

Our Father in heaven, Hallowed be your name   Your kingdom come your will be done on earth as it is in heaven

Give us today our daily bread.

And forgive us our debts, as we also have forgiven our debtors.

And lead us not into temptation, but deliver us from the evil one:

(Narrator: After the prayer, Kim tells everyone that they can take a seat, but she notices that one of the guys who was fighting last time is still standing. This makes her curious and nervous at the same time, but she figures she should at least make sure to ask him if he is all right[YE66] [MF67] . Besides, there is extra security in the room.

Charles: Excuse me, your name is Kim, right? I would really like to apologize to you and everyone who was here last time for causing so much trouble and interrupting you. I didn't want to accept the information that you were trying to deliver. I have never had anyone talk to me about Jesus until I met James.

Kim: Wow. I'm sorry to hear that. But I'm glad you decided to come back to the chapel so that you can hear a little more, if you're interested.

Charles: Again, I just wanted to apologize to you today, and I'm glad to be here. Thank you.

Kim: Is it okay for me to teach you all a song?

(Oh, clap your hands, everybody!

Everybody should praise the Lord.

For the Lord thy God is awesome,

And he's the king over all of everything

[Repeat]

Oh, come let us sing for him loud! Let us shout for our rock, our Jesus!

Let us come filled with thanksgiving So let
us shout hallelujah amen repeat

Oh, come let us worship and bow,

And let us kneel before our maker.

For he is God today and always,

So let us shout hallelujah, amen!

[Repeat chorus]

So sing praise, sing to our God,

Sing praise, sing praise to our King,

Sing praise, sing praise to Jesus,

for he's over all of everything.

[Repeat chorus])

After singing the song, she goes to her Bible and begins reading from Matthew 13:15–17 (KJV): For this people's heart has become calloused, they hardly hear with their ears, and they have closed their eyes Otherwise they might see with their eyes, hear with ears, understand with their hearts and turn, and I would heal them.

Kim: Does anyone have any questions about what we just read from the Bible?

Charles raises his hand and says, "I think I might understand what this might mean."

Kim: Okay, Charles. Go ahead and tell us what you think.

Charles looks over at James, who seems shocked that things are going so well. He encourages Charles to give an answer as well. So Charles says, "I believe that he is saying that if people open their eyes and ears and take in the lessons of the Bible, God will most likely help them; otherwise, they will never be healed."

Kim: Yes, Charles, that is correct, but that is why it is so important to accept Christ as your savior. That's why we have to open our ears, eyes, and hearts so that we can get some real understanding of the lessons from the Bible.

Kim asks everyone if they understand. Everyone says yes.

Kim: I'm going to close with a prayer.

James stands up and asks if it's okay if he does it. Kim says, "Sure. I really don't see why not."

James: Father God, I'd first like to say thank you for allowing everyone to be here today to hear your words, especially Charles. Lord, I want to thank you for giving us the message of opening our eyes, ears, and hearts so that we may all have the opportunity to grow closer to you, Heavenly Father. I'd also like to pray for forgiveness of my sins and a chance for me to personally do better, Lord. In the name of your son, Jesus Christ, amen.

After chapel, Kim approaches James and Charles. She lets them know that it was a pleasure having them at chapel and offers them a card for her church just in case they are released before she is allowed to come back. They both accept the cards and thank her again.

A FEW MONTHS LATER

Both Charles and James receive great news. Their charges have been dropped. They both had to appear before a judge. Because it was Charles' first offense, the judge gave him 72 hours of community service.

James ended up getting released and placed on an ankle bracelet for 72 hours.

Scene Ten

Two weeks after being released, Charles contacts Kim about checking out the church. Kim gives Charles the directions to the church and asks that he be there on the first Sunday at 10:30 a.m. Charles thanks Kim for the information, and they end their conversation. Afterward, Charles calls James and lets him know what Kim said, and they agree to attend the service.

AT THE CHURCH

Service is starting. The pastor is opening up church [YE68] [MF69] with a prayer and then the song "Let the Church Say Amen." [YE70] [MF71] Kim gets a text from Charles, saying that he's going to be about 15 minutes late. Kim says okay. Church goes on into testimony service, and Kim starts praising the Lord, saying what he did in her life. How she finally got some people to hear the word of Father God.

Ashley shows up and sits down. Kim has started singing the song and almost lets go[YE72] [MF73] . Ashley joins her in singing a song by Kurt Carr.[YE74] [MF75]

Charles finally arrives.

Charles thinks to himself that this cannot be happening for real. He is in total shock. People praising the Lord, saying thank you Jesus—he hasn't seen anything like this before.

James sees the look on Charles' face and asks him if he is all right.

Charles: I have never been to church, and I have never seen anything like this before.

After the song, Pastor Willie Stevens starts preaching the word of God. Psalm 121:1–8 and 100:1–5. An hour later, the love offering was passed around. The church has a special guest—a gospel rap recording artist, who sings his new gospel hit, "Shout It Out" (check out reform productions on YouTube). The pastor blesses the artist with the church offering. He then closes the church with a prayer.

OUTSIDE THE CHURCH

Kim: Ashley, come over. I would like you to meet somebody. His name is James. He is one of the guys in jail I met when speaking about the good Lord.

Ashley, it's a pleasure to meet you. [YE76] [MF77]

Charles (looking for Kim): James.

Charles: Hey, Kim.

Kim: Hey, Charles, glad you made it.

Charles: Service was great.

Kim: Glad you enjoy the service. I would like you to meet someone else. She's like a sister to me. Her name is Ashley. Ashley!

As Ashley gets closer, her heart starts beating fast.

Charles: Is Ashley who I think it is?

Kim: You know my friend?

Ashley (*screams*): Kim, get over here now!

Kim: Excuse me, Charles, I'll be right back.

Ashley: Girl, you know that's the guy I was telling you about! That's the guy who beat me! That's him! His name is Charles.

Kim (*in a loud voice*): What?

*Charles walks over to Kim, and
Ashley starts panicking.*

Charles: Is everything all right?

Kim: Now I see what you were going through in the situation you were in. You hit my best friend. I'm about to crack your fucking face in.

Ashley: No, Kim, I got this. Charles, you have the nerve to come around here after what you did to me. Are you crazy?

Charles: Ashley, I didn't know what was going on in my head. I thought you were cheating on me with a guy Jesus.

Ashley: Ha ha.

Charles: Really, when I was growing up, people didn't teach me about Jesus. I'm very sorry, Ashley, if I hurt you in any way[YE78] [MF79] . I'm sorry for my actions.

Ashley: Wow, how do you know about Jesus now?

Charles: My trusty friend, James, helped me through the journey. All praises.

Kim: I was there the whole time.

Charles: Thank you, Kim, for your time. So, Ashley, I still love you, but I will give you time to renew our friendship again.

Ashley: Charles, I will always love you. If you need to talk, my number is the same.

Charles: Thanks, Ashley.

James came out of the church

James: Charles, give me a verse.

Charles: I feel my Lord will listen to thisGalatians 5:22-23 But the fruit of the Spirit is love, joy, peace, patience, kindness, goodness, faithfulness, gentleness, and self-control. Against such things there is no law.

 [YE80] James: All praises, brother. That's what I call awareness

YEARS LATER

Finally, Ashley and Charles get back together, studying, dating, and much more. They decide to get married.

Charles and Ashley exchange vowels, and they get married happily.

James studies on his own. He hasn't been back to church.

People, wake up, pick up your Bibles, find out about your savior, and rejoice in his name. Amen.

THE END

ALL BIBLE VERSES ARE FROMTHE
HOLY BIBLE
NEW INTERNATIONAL VERSION
THE NIV
RAINBOW STUDY BIBLE
BOLD LINE COLOR CODED EDITION
GUIDEPOSTS

[YE1] It seems that James doesn't have a dedicated background sheet. Consider adding this to ensure consistency. This way, readers will also gain a better understanding of his personality.

[MF2]yes

[MF3]yes

[MF4]yes

[YE5]As these are common nouns, these have been changed from title case to lower case. Per *CMoS* 5.5, common nouns are not capitalized unless they begin a sentence or appear in a title.

[MF6]yes

[YE7]Per *CMoS* 9.2, "In nontechnical contexts, Chicago advises spelling out whole numbers from zero through one hundred and certain round multiples of those numbers." This rule applies to cardinal as well as ordinal numbers.

[MF8]yes

[YE9]Per *CMoS* 6.24, a dependent clause that precedes a main clause should be followed by a comma.

[MF10]yes

[YE11]Per *CMoS* 6.22, when independent clauses are joined by *and, but, or, so, yet, for,* or any other coordinating conjunction, a comma usually precedes the conjunction.

[MF12]yes

[YE13]Per *CMoS* 8.92, "Alternative or descriptive names for God as supreme being are capitalized.

Adonai

the Almighty

the Deity

the Holy Ghost or the Holy Spirit or the Paraclete

the Lord

Providence

the Supreme Being

the Trinity"

[MF14]yes

[YE15]To ensure that the headings are consistent, such scene descriptions have been placed after the heading.

[MF16]yes

[YE17]To ensure consistency in spelling, *okay* has been used throughout the book.

[MF18]yes

[YE19]Per *CMoS* 6.63, when a colon introduces two or more sentences or when it introduces speech in dialogue or a quotation or question, the first word following it is capitalized.

[MF20]yes

[YE21]A comma after "so" is not necessary if it functions as a conjunction. However, when "so" is used as an interjection, a comma can be added, depending on whether there is a natural pause at that point.

[MF22]yes

[YE23]Per *CMoS* 6.53, "A comma is used to set off names or words used in direct address."

[MF24]yes

[YE25]Although this type of construction is nonstandard and against grammatical rules, such constructions have been retained to add flavor to the character.

[MF26]yes

[YE27]*Their* is the possessive form of *they*, so it has to do with what belongs to, relates to, or is made or done by certain people, animals, or things:

It's their house.
We're their neighbors.
The trees are losing their leaves.

They're is a contraction that means "they are."

They're (=they are) funny people.
They're (=they are) the cutest puppies ever.

Here, "they're" is correct.

[MF28]yes

[YE29]Instead of including this information within three separate sets of parentheses, consider including this as three separate paragraphs within one set of parentheses. This is because using consecutive parentheses is usually not preferred in writing.

[MF30]yes

[YE31]For better word choice, consider using "making these overly nice gestures."

[MF32]yes

[YE33]*You're* is a contraction of the phrase *you are*. *Your* is a possessive adjective used to show ownership. It is not a contraction. *Your* is usually followed by a noun.

In this section, *you're* is correct.

[MF34]yes

[YE35]Edited to avoid repetition.

[MF36]yes

[YE37]Per *CMoS* 8.103, "Names of scriptures and other highly revered works are capitalized but not usually italicized (except when used in the title of a published work)."

[MF38]yes

[YE39]Edited to correct syntax.

[MF40]yes

[YE41]The scene description seems to be present for some scenes and missing for others. To ensure consistency, consider including scene descriptions for all scenes.

[MF42]yrs

[YE43]Per *CMoS* 7.16 and 7.17, the possessive of most singular nouns is formed by adding an apostrophe and an s. The possessive of plural nouns (except for a few irregular plurals, like children, that do not end in s) is formed by adding an apostrophe only. This general rule extends to the possessives of proper nouns, including names ending in s, x, or z, in both their singular and plural forms, as well as abbreviations and numbers.

[MF44]yes

[YE45]Consider deleting this to avoid repetition.

[MF46]yes

[YE47]Times should be rendered in numerals with "a.m." and "p.m." when exact times are important. The format must be 0:00 p.m.

[MF48]yes

[YE49]Please note that from this point onward, scene/narrative descriptions do not start with "Narrator." Please consider including them to ensure consistency. Alternatively, you can remove "Narrator" from all scene descriptions.

[MF50]Please keep that in to keep everything the same throughout

[YE51]Edited for better syntax.

[MF52]yes

[YE53]To ensure consistency, please enclose all scene descriptions within parentheses or remove the parentheses around all of them.

[MF54]yes

[YE55]Added to improve syntax.

[MF56]yes

[YE57]Edited to improve syntax.

[MF58]yes

[YE59]Consider adding "Charles" at the beginning to indicate that this monologue is by him.

[MF60]yes

[YE61]It seems that this verse hasn't been cited. If so, please consider providing a parenthetical citation for it.

[MF62]delete

[YE63]It seems that this verse hasn't been cited. If so, please consider providing a parenthetical citation for it.

[YE64]To ensure that the identity of the speaker is clear, consider adding the following at the beginning of this line: "James muses, "I wish…"

[MF65]James wasn't speaking to anyone. He was just having a private thought

[YE66]Per *Merriam-Webster*, the correct spelling is "all right."

[MF67]Yes

[YE68] [YE68]Per *CMoS* 8.98, "When used to refer to the institution of religion or of a particular religion, church is usually lowercased unless a particular author or publisher prefers otherwise." Moreover, "*Church* is capitalized when part of the formal name of a denomination or congregation."

[MF69]yes

[YE70]Per *CMoS* 8.194, "Titles of songs and other shorter musical compositions are set in roman and enclosed in quotation marks, capitalized in the same way as poems."

[MF71]By marvin winans

[YE72]This seems vague. Consider rephrasing this with different wording.

[MF73]yes

[YE74]Edited for improved syntax.

[MF75]Yes

[YE76]Who says this? Consider naming the speaker before the dialogue.

[MF77]Ashley

[YE78]A better choice in this context would be "I'm very sorry, Ashley, that I hurt you." Consider implementing this.

[MF79]yes

[YE80]If this is a verse from the Bible, consider including a citation for it in the dialogue.

Ingram Content Group UK Ltd.
Milton Keynes UK
UKHW021828250723
425770UK00016B/740